Reflec
Showing Up As You
Are (put in a book for
no reason)

Zahra Jaffer

BookLeaf
Publishing

Reflections On Showing Up As You Are
(put in a book for no reason) © 2022 Zahra
Jaffer

All rights reserved.

Presentation by *BookLeaf Publishing*

Web: www.bookleafpub.com

E-mail: info@bookleafpub.com

ISBN: 9789357617505

First edition 2022

PREFACE

Notes for people feeling lost in this individualistic society, and some reflections on how to find a way out. These poems are about healing during complicated times. It shows you a way to be active and conscious. For me, it was the perfect way to consolidate a few years of hard work and lots of meaningful conversations with loved ones.

You are not just 1 thing

Who do you think you are?
Do you know who I am?

The self can only take you so far,
You should learn from others, see where you
land.

In this world of worshiping the self,
And the pressure to be the high-functioning
individual.

How do you value yourself?
Do you count all your achievements?
If no one has congratulated you, well done.
They all count.
Be proud of yourself.
You are everything!

Showing yourself love is the basic requirement
for progress,
Speak kind words because you are doing great.
When you are ready,
you can do more.

True self-love is not frivolous,

It requires you to recommit daily

You can not look outward for the lessons on how to do it,
This is personal to you.

Remember you are allowed to make mistakes,
It is part of the journey.

Remember you are allowed to say the wrong thing,
As long as you commit to learning and growing.

Remember change is part of the process,
Flickering between different states of being,
Every year trying to be brand new.

Forever questioning Who am I, Who is this,
Am I ready to find out?

The origin of your energy

They say it's all energy,
It is all around us and affecting us in ways we
wouldn't believe.

What I have learnt about my own energy,
Came from lessons learnt whilst dancing around
the uncontrollable energy of others.

Remember your words can transmute the energy
of this world,
They say even when it is difficult you should
lead with love.

Without letting go of the past and your ideas of
self,
There can be no spiritual wealth.

There can be no spiritual wealth,
Only good energy and good vibes.

There can be no spiritual wealth,
But there are benefits to seeking spiritual
knowledge.

There can be no spiritual wealth and you won't
be doing it for gains,
But to lighten the load on your soul.

There can be no spiritual wealth,
Not in this realm.

The wealth you gain from your own spiritual
journey
Will be felt in the energy that you bring to a
room.

The spiritual one is careful with their words,
They are considering what they watch and what
they consume.

How do we become like this?
We are pulled in so many directions in this
modern world.
How can we strengthen the spirit?

It isn't easy to admit your behaviours may be a
result of your past,
That is step one.
Remember your childhood. Who were you?
How did you feel?

There is a part of the process that involves
acceptance,

Accept the wounds of your childhood,
Remember the unmet needs,
Consider how they shape you.
There is power in looking into your past for the
moments that conditioned you.
Can you forgive the people who have hurt you?
Can you give them the benefit of the doubt?

You cannot truly show up as you are if you are
weighed down the past,
We know letting go is important.
How many of us are holding onto pain?

Remember your childhood. Who were you?
How did you feel?
Your youthful and playful side is your
superpower,
Find the things that draw that youthful energy
out of you.
Reignite your desire to learn.

We are all children,
Even the elders in your own life,
Our souls are young,
And need to be cared for.

Emotions come in waves of positive and
negative,

There is an overwhelming amount of stimulus
directing this movement within the Self.

Feeling not good enough is just a feeling,
Watch it as it crashes over you.
Don't let it move you,
Your rationality might save you from being
swallowed by these waves.
Sometimes.

It is difficult to be unmoved by a thing in the
present,
Especially if it reminds you of the past.
That was then,
This is now.

Ups and Downs,
They come and go.
Remind yourself that you got through the bad,
You made it all the way to some good moments,
it is all a journey.

Remember who you were before,
You started working to protect yourself from
others.
Remember the curiosity.
Bring it into the present.

Recognise how your past has impacted your
present,
Then let it go.
Only then will you have the strength to go
forward,
And the world needs you.
We need the energy that you bring.
It is why you are here.

Don't hesitate

Are you afraid of this world?
I wouldn't blame you if you were.

There are no bad people,
There is just confrontation, and that's scary.

There are no bad people,
There are just conflicting ideologies.

There are no bad people,
But this world is suffering at the hands of human
beings hiding behind corporations.

There is not anything to be afraid of,
Fear is actually pretty detrimental to your
progress.

People will tell you being cautious is wise,
Whatever you believe, do not let caution stifle
you.

In the realm of your passions,
A moment of hesitation is dangerous.

The consequences are always unknown,

No matter how hard you try.

You must reflect,
Enquire into why you hide your Self.
Dive deeper and enquire into what is holding
you back.

Do you even know what you desire?
Is it influenced by the culture of today?
Or do you know how to listen to your own
heart?

Make movements.

Only you know your natural Self

Water your plants
Water your Self.

The eb and flow of the self is a beautiful thing,
Try not to get too attached to who you are.

Search for your own truth without
self-righteousness,
Remember that no one path looks the same.
There is nothing to be gained from judging
others.

Relationships are important for your future,
But you are the most important part of your
future.
Pay attention to yourself.

What brings you joy?
Ask yourself every day,
and notice how it changes with age.
Every day is a blessing.
I hope you see it that way.

Talking to the Ego

Have you ever tried to get to know your own
ego?
I have, and I am not alone.

We all need to understand our ego,
We need to be able to feel our own resistance.

We can then move through it,
Towards our truth and our essence, who we may
have never known.
We may have silenced our essence when we
were young.
It does not matter anymore,
All we can do is try to reclaim it.

There is only now,
The past is nothing but a lesson.

Start noticing when your words aren't your own
Your conditioning is showing itself to you and to
the world.
Other people see it, so you must learn to.

If we take away our individual attachments,
And we are all the same.

We have the same basic needs,
With very different means.
Remember we all have weaknesses.
And we need each other.

Don't worry about how people view you,
You cannot control it.
Only worry about what you can do today.

Your ego will try to disturb your peace,
It is invested in the actions of others.
Your ego will have you self-sabotaging,
and your essence will fade away.

You have to take ownership of your own peace,
The impressions that make up your ego will
steal your essence,
If you let them.
Dedicate yourself to changing.

In the pits of anger we often lose ourselves,
We misplace our honourable intentions,
The ego demonstrates its power.

Stay calm.
Keep your own peace.

Take action and Be free

If you really listen to yourself, you yearn for
freedom not for worldly possessions.

There is freedom in the pursuit of your goals,
Reflect on your goals and remind yourself of
your power.

Freedom is our divine right,
The politicians have convoluted how we
understand it.
If you want the truth, look at the concept with a
philosopher.

In a way, having a lack of expectations is a form
of freedom,
Allowing you to be in an unrestrained pursuit of
your purpose.

The soul desires freedom to express itself,
It is not moved by worldly possessions.
We are more than consumers,
And we must remember that.

Is self-preservation your focus?
Aren't you tired?

Forever committed to chasing that which you
cannot control.
Do you feel free?

I believe there is freedom in the pursuit of your
goals,
So action your dreams.

Comfort is not freedom.
Trust that your essence will guide you,
So long as you do not commit to hiding.

Your mind may make mountains out of
moments,
Learn to trust your path.
Always do your best.
Everything will be okay.

Don't worship your own rationale,
Always seek council.
Every day we are affected by moments we don't
even remember.

Make your actions for you.
You are the most important thing in your life.

Your spirit will try to show you your truth,
It is your role to implement it into your reality.
You do this by honouring your Self.

So start listening to yourself,
Try get clear on what you actually want.

Add fuel to your own fire,
It isn't about productivity,
It is about passion.
At least it should be.

It is time for action,
You can't imprison your essence any longer,
Especially not in your own mind.
You have to show up.
You have to show the world.

Intuition is divine and Rationale is man-made

We live in a post-enlightenment world,
Where we believe reason rules it all.

Internally our intuition and our reason battle it
out,
Although the battle is in a time warp.
The past dominates your rationale,
Your intuition lives in the moment
And in your body.

Your mind is in a tug of war,
There are different sides of your self that are
calling to be integrated.
Find your own balance,
There is truth there.
Listen to yourself.

You can only move with purpose when you have
aligned these parts,
By being committed to truly understanding them
for what they are.

There are multiple ways to utilise your essence,

Pay attention to what feels fulfilling in the
moment.

Your truth lives within your hopes and dreams,
Your conditioning and self-esteem may cause
you to doubt your primal instincts.
The truth is a matter of the soul.

The modern world has gone too far,
To feel fulfilled you might need to refresh your
own mind,
Get back to the body and soul.

You know nothing

Sacrifice your ideas about yourself to the altar of
your Self.
If not in the name of God, then in the name of
Progress.

You will find your truth when you let go of your
attachments.
There is no space for self-entitlement on this
journey,
and being sensitive will be sacrificed for the
sake of collaboration.

Seeking love and approval can be painful,
you must look within for validation.
Most of us do not know what will make us
happy,
we don't even know ourselves fully.

Authenticity is fluid

Be Authentic,
But be here for your fellow citizen.

You are here to serve, this is not a belief
reserved for the pious,
It is built into your nature and essential to our
ecosystem.

Our species dying, crying and lying.
We are all the same species inhabiting a
decaying rock

We don't all watch the same news and the same
shows,
Is anyone else thinking about their virtues?
I often wonder, am I virtuous or a tyrant?
Aren't we all a bit of both - taking turns to show
that side.

Do you consciously try to be good?
Do you consider your life to be a good life?

We are all on a journey that no one can see,
I think we are all just tired.

I want to know how I can show up as myself
here,
I want to know how we can be of service to one
another.

So much energy going into who I become,
not enough consideration for how I can serve.

It is a feeling, not a thought

Does the mind always deserve to decide?
Do you allow yourself to be moved?

Your mind might not always be your friend, we
ruminate.

Your experiences may have given you wisdom,
they also came with scars.
Don't sacrifice your essence
To the whispers of your pain.

Our generation only has time for cursory
research,
you could ask me why for hours and hours,
I would say there is no time for unnecessary
enquiry.

Ask your Self.

Discover power in the darkness

The shadow self is important,
Have you heard of it?

Exploring the shadow is a practice in
discovering how powerful you are,
You have to honour all of your Self to
understand your essence.

Without developing knowledge of Self,
You won't be able to break your patterns.

You must look at the shadow before you can
truly show up in the world,
When I did, I found a new understanding of
myself.
If you fail to integrate the shadow self,
You'll find problems that seem to be someone
else's fault.

It is an opportunity to use Truth,
And to harness the power to change.
You have the strength to break well-entrenched
patterns.
To truly show up, you have to do the work.

Your strengths weigh more than your struggles,
shadow-work is an opportunity to shift anything
that is out of alignment.

There is no search for perfection when looking
at the self.
The process of getting to know oneself,
it has been compromised.
It no longer feels spiritual.
It has been influenced by Capitalism,
Now we are told to optimise and not to feel.

There is no search for perfection when looking
at the self.
We have been encouraged to hide for
generations,
whilst we get the job done.
Now we curate our Self for the latest social
media,
and continue to consume.

The places within that you must go to
in order to discover your true power are dark.
It involves confronting your shadows,
And admitting where you have caused pain.
Taking yourself on a journey,
where you can finally commit to a new form of
light.

You cannot tightly hold onto your pain,
It will make you envious and competitive.
It will make you susceptible to a fragile sense of
self,
One that is far too common these days.

Spend some time getting to know your own
essence,
then make some plans for yourself.
In the name of self-love,
Start to fill your life with things that make you
smile.

Every day you reach the same crossroad,
Where you choose how to live.
You must choose to live for your future self.
Release the idea that you need to self-sacrifice,
The comfort of others is not your concern.
Bravery is the antidote to any stagnation.

Once you bring awareness to the shadow,
You can learn to accept yourself,
This will naturally open your heart to others,
And give you the power to show up as you are.

There is no need to hide,
you are made of light.

Purpose and Spirituality

Once you truly start to recognise yourself,
Learn about your own intentions and patterns,
you may find yourself drawn to help others.

This world has become an darker with every
year that I have existed,
Yet we have more options than ever before.
Your light is needed here.

The internet has provided me with so much,
Yet it takes my vital attention every day.
Where does your active attention go?

If financial gain is your main goal,
Then you are further from your soul than you
realise.
You could be pious and good,
But if you aren't helping thy neighbour, what is
it worth?
This help does not refer to financial aid.

As humans we have more purpose than our
consumption,
as a collective we seem to have forgotten that.

We are the only species who pay to live on this planet.

Do you know your own limit?
Do you know that we are running on limited resources?
How much suffering can you witness?
Albeit from a distance.
Can you feel the withering of your spirit?

Be more than just a consumer,
Or a unique individual.
Dedicate yourself to contributing in a meaningful way.

This starts by feeding your own soul,
Finding what drives you.

Are you true to your values?
Do you know what the principles that guide you are?
Start there,
and find yourself closer to your Purpose.

Innovate

Capitalism brought us the technology that
transformed our lives,
both positively and negatively.
It is responsible for many of the advancements
we see.
It cannot fix our current societal problems.
It is a global issue,
that we view as nationalists.

The inequality gap widens,
and the masses are misguided.
Like confused cattle we are moved
from news story to new story.
We accept that there are separate rule books,
for the individual and the corporations.
We accept.

There seems to be no love for the fellow human,
Only rules and conventions that we follow.
We need a new collective system of ethics,
Who wants to talk about that?

I am learning to be patient with loved ones,
they are all human first and foremost.
We don't all have to believe the same thing,

but we have to be able to discuss it.
Let us learn from each other.

Let us innovate our own lives.
Let's call it a social evolution,
Not a revolution.
Then the Conservatives might still feel safe.

What level of change is required?
What should the activists be aspiring to change?
Given everything that we now know...
What do you feel needs to change?
Everything.

Being an individual wasn't working for me,
I seek community and I seek to be of service.
The truth is, it is humbling.
I am nothing but a moment in the journey of
human-kind.
It would be an honour to contribute in a
meaningful way.

Listen to yourself

Listening to yourself,
and listening to your Self.
It is easier said than done,
please take time alone and away
from noise of this world.

Show love, be honest
and set boundaries in the present.
Learn about your material needs,
And your own requirements for a peaceful Self.

Meet yourself again, as a body.
You are not simply this concept of self,
That your ego uses to drive you around.

You are an essence that lives in your body,
Feel into that every now and then.
Practice listening to that.

Be grateful for your body,
As it houses your soul.
Listen to your body,
It sends you signals.

If you are overwhelmed with emotion,

Notice how your body feels and what it is doing.
Welcome presence into your life,
Simply by listening to yourself.

Why am I wrote this down

Life is a little bit like an experiment,
We are all just test subjects
Adding new variables.
We have been experimenting for our entire
existence.

It is all a shared human experience.
Find wisdom in the Lessons of History.
Learn from your peers.

I think we should all try to learn from each other
more,
I am dropping any f*ck the hater nonsense and
moving
Towards a proper consideration of how I show
up.

When you feel the weight of the past
And the pressure of the future pushing you,
Taking you further away from your Self.
Feel the warmth of possibility in the present,
Remember the messages from your own essence
And let go of the rest.

It is why I put pen to paper,
I am just trialing a new mode of being.
I felt compelled to write.
I hope you like...

How?

Wherever you go in the material world,
do what you can to be close to your spirit.
Do whatever it takes to bring your spirit peace.

Notice how things feel in your body,
How they stir your soul.

Every day we learn about ourselves,
We meet new versions of the Self.
Each fragment of Self resides in our essence,
It is a beautiful thing.

The Self that was not allowed to flourish,
Yet continues to show itself
in hopes that you change your ways.

Rest

Remember to rest.
Remember to take rest,
and to honour where you are.

The hardest times have been when
I put unnecessary pressure on myself.
Learn from that mistake.
Learn to ask for help.

We are all struggling in our own way,
until the end comes.
Be supportive and love everyone,
And always have fun.

Listen to yourself,
Your body will tell you
To take rest.

Be realistic with your expectation of others,
Take ownership of your life.
Take rest
And celebrate when you can.

Reflection matters

Your patterns aren't holding you prisoner,
They are trying to keep you safe.

Your inner being is confused about who takes
care of it,
You are the only one who can take care of your
Self.
First you must know your Self.

I put these words together,
composed from my own journals
I have presented my recent reflections,
Trying to make it make sense.

I cannot stress the importance of looking back,
I did it to learn.
I desired to grow.

How can you make sure you are reflecting and
not regretting?
It is tough, the past is complicated.
I would say the differentiating factor is hope for
the future.
Hope is the key to positive reflection

Write it down your own reflections.
It will give you a unique clarity and
understanding
Of your own essence.

Gain awareness of your Self,
So that you can start following the paths that
make you feel alive.

When you look back at your life,
You must do it with absolute trust in your future.
I believe they call it manifesting.

What I am trying to say is
Reflecting is the first step to moving forward.

When you reflect,
You must be willing to own up to your actions,
Remember how you have showed up in the past.

You can work with the different parts of your
Self,
And create a new present.
It will require a willingness to examine the past.

Make the effort to understand why you are the
way you are,
Then hopefully you won't need a professional to
explain it to you.

Reflect on your Self,
Like the sun shines on the moon,
Illuminating new sides every night.

Be kind and true,
to your Self and to others.

We are all just searching for peace.
So show up as you are
And don't be afraid.
Reflect on that.

Ingram Content Group UK Ltd.
Milton Keynes UK
UKHW020719200423
420491UK00015B/583

9 789357 617505